Pursuing a
Deeper Faith

BY

Charles F. Stanley

Thomas Nelson
Since 1798

NASHVILLE   DALLAS   MEXICO CITY   RIO DE JANEIRO

Published in Nashville, Tennessee, by Thomas Nelson, Inc.

Editing, design, and typesetting by Gregory C. Benoit Publishing, Old Mystic, CT.

Scripture quotations are from THE NEW KING JAMES VERSION. Copyright ©
1979, 1980, 1982, Thomas Nelson, Inc., Publishers.

ISBN 9781418544201

1 2 3 4 14 13 12 11

Contents

Preparing for Growth

Each of us has a perspective on the world and on life—a way of looking at things, of judging things, of holding things in the memory. We need to recognize that our perspective is something that we have learned, and we need to recognize that we may have adopted a wrong understanding about certain things.

I have found in my years of ministry that a wrong perspective is very common when it comes to spiritual growth. A faulty perspective about God can be a major stumbling block toward an intimate relationship with God. For example, a person who believes God to be a harsh and angry judge is likely to shy away from having a relationship with Him. A person who believes God to be the only source of unconditional love and abundant grace is likely to seek an ever-deepening relationship with Him.

Similarly, what we believe about Jesus is likely to limit or define the degree to which we become like Him in character; and that, in turn, will determine the limits that we place on our own spiritual growth.

The Bible is our authority when it comes to the nature of God and how to have an intimate relationship with Him. It is our authority when it comes to our spiritual growth. Therefore, it is the reference to which we must return continually to compare what we *believe* with what God *desires* for us. Our perspective is wrong if it doesn't match up with God's eternal truth.

This book can be used by you alone or by several people in a small-group study. At various times, you will be asked to relate to the material in one of these four ways:

1. *What new insights have you gained?* Make notes about the insights that you have. You may want to record them in your Bible or in a separate journal. As you reflect back over your insights, you are likely to see how God has moved in your life.

2. *Have you ever had a similar experience?* Each of us approaches the Bible from a unique background—our own particular set of relationships and experiences. Our experiences do not make the Bible true—the Word of God is truth regardless of our opinion about it. It is important, however, to share our experiences in order to see how God's truth can be applied to human lives.

3. *How do you feel about the material presented?* Emotional responses do not give validity to the Scriptures, nor should we trust our emotions as a gauge for our faith. In small-group Bible study, however, it is good for participants to express their emotions. The Holy Spirit often communicates with us through this unspoken language.

4. *In what way do you feel challenged to respond or to act?* God's Word may cause you to feel inspired or challenged to change something in your life. Take the challenge seriously and find ways of acting upon it. If God reveals to you a particular need that He wants *you* to address, take that as "marching orders" from God. God is expecting you to *do* something with the challenge that He has just given you.

Start and conclude your Bible study sessions in prayer. Ask God to give you spiritual eyes to see and spiritual ears to hear. As you conclude your study, ask the Lord to seal what you have learned so that you will never forget it. Ask Him to help you grow into the fullness of the stature of Christ Jesus.

Again, I caution you to keep the Bible at the center of your study. A genuine Bible study stays focused on God's Word and promotes a growing faith and a closer walk with the Holy Spirit in *each* person who participates.

LESSON 1

God's Invitation

❧ In This Lesson ❧

LEARNING: WHAT IS THE DIFFERENCE BETWEEN KNOWING GOD AND KNOW-
ING ABOUT GOD?

GROWING: HOW CAN I COME TO KNOW GOD?

Our heavenly Father has issued to each of us a very special two-part invitation. The first part of the invitation is to *know* Him. We are invited to know *about* our heavenly Father, and also to *know Him*: to be in intimate, personal, relationship with Him, and to experience His presence in an ongoing, daily way.

The Invitation to Know God

There is a vast difference between knowing *about* God and *knowing God*. To know about God is to have a head-knowledge of God—to believe that He exists and to draw conclusions about His nature. To know about God is to have an understanding of God and the way in which He works, the commandments that He has given for living, and the plan that He has implemented for our eternal salvation through Jesus Christ, His Son.

To actually *know* God is something quite different. It is to have a heart relationship with God—to experience His presence and to hear His voice speaking in your spirit on a daily basis, guiding you into the right paths and the right decisions that He desires for you. It is to have a deep assurance that you are locked into a relationship with Him forever, a relationship that cannot be severed by anything that you or another person might do. It is to have confidence of God's love and presence with you always.

You may know a great deal *about* another person—his name, age, height, color of eyes, occupation, church affiliation, some of his historical background, and so forth. But if you only know the basic facts and figures of that person's life, then you don't really know him on a personal level. To know a person is to know what makes him laugh and what brings tears to his eyes. It is to share experiences with him, to spend time with him and to converse with him personally and privately—both talking and listening as you exchange confidences, opinions, dreams, and struggles.

We cannot, of course, fully know God; He can never be fully fathomed, known, or loved. He is infinite in His power, wisdom, love, and presence, while we are finite—and the finite can never fully understand the infinite. But we *can* know Him better and better. We *can* experience a deeper and deeper relationship with God.

> That I may know Him and the power of His resurrection, and the fellowship of His sufferings, being conformed to His death, if, by any means, I may attain to the resurrection from the dead.
>
> —Philippians 3:10, 11

↞ What does it mean to know God? According to these verses, what are some of the results of knowing God?

↞ According to these verses, what are some of the costs of knowing God? What might be involved in this process?

The Invitation to Become Like Jesus

The second part of God's invitation to each of us is an invitation to become more like Jesus Christ day by day. Many people believe that all the Lord desires for us is that we be born again—that we accept Jesus Christ as our personal Savior and then continue to believe in Him until the day when we die and go to heaven. The Lord most certainly desires this for each of us, but He wants *so much more!*

Many people are saved, but it's as if they crossed the threshold into salvation and then never took another step. Our life in Christ does not end with a salvation experience. That is only the beginning point. Spiritual growth is to be the norm of our lives, every day of our lives.

In our relationship with the Lord, we are invited to grow spiritually so that we are continually becoming more like Christ Jesus in our character, which in turn is manifested in behavior. Who we are as people is continually to be displayed in how we think and respond to life, what we say, and what we do.

We are to bear the identity of the Holy Spirit at work in us, displaying His fruit: love, joy, peace, patience, kindness, goodness, faithfulness, gentleness, and self-control (see Gal. 5:22, 23). We are to respond to needs as Jesus would respond—with power and love and mercy. We are to think what Jesus would think in response to every situation that we encounter, and to say what He would say.

We can never become fully like Jesus in this lifetime. But we are invited— yes, called and challenged—to become *more like* Jesus every day. We are to continue to grow into the fullness of His character.

> For whom He foreknew, He also predestined to be conformed to the image of His Son, that He might be the firstborn among many brethren.
>
> —Romans 8:29

What does it mean to "be conformed to the image" of Jesus? How is this done? What are the results?

What does it mean that Jesus is "the firstborn among many brethren"? What does this imply about *your* relationship to God?

A Lifetime Challenge

Our quest to have an ever-deepening relationship with our heavenly Father, and our growth into the fullness of Christ's character, is a lifetime challenge. We never reach perfection in our spiritual growth. Neither are we to rest on a plateau of spiritual maturity. We must never assume that we know God as well as we can know Him or that we are as spiritually mature as the Lord wants us to be.

There's always room for greater growth and a deeper relationship with the Lord.

Today and Tomorrow

TODAY: CHRISTIANS ARE CALLED TO KNOW GOD IN AN INTIMATE, LOVING RELATIONSHIP.

TOMORROW: I WILL SPEND TIME THIS WEEK ASKING GOD TO TEACH ME HOW TO BECOME MORE LIKE JESUS.

Notes and Prayer Requests:

Are You Growing? (Part 1)

What evidence do you have that you are growing spiritually? Do you have a means of evaluating spiritual growth? Many people who attend church just go through the motions. They may even pray and read their Bibles daily, but they have no evidence of growth or of changes in their life that are linked to their spirituality. Fewer still have an understanding about how to recognize signs of spiritual growth. If you find yourself in one of those categories, this lesson is for you.

God's Call to Growth

God's Word challenges us to grow. Spiritual growth is not an option or a nice idea—it is a commandment. Our lives in Christ should exhibit a continual and steady growth. In 2 Peter 3:17, 18 we read:

> You therefore, beloved. . . beware lest you also fall from your own steadfastness, being led away with the error of the wicked; but grow in the grace and knowledge of our Lord and Savior Jesus Christ.

☙ What does it mean to "fall from your own steadfastness"? To what are Christians called to be steadfast? How does one fall from that?

☙ How does a person "grow in the grace and knowledge of our Lord and Savior Jesus Christ"? In what ways does such growth help one to be steadfast?

Do We "Grow" into Salvation?

Some people respond to the question, "Are you born again?" by saying, "No, not yet, but I'm growing into it." Of one thing we can be certain— we do not *grow* into salvation. A person is either saved or not saved. A person is never "almost" saved or "about to be" saved as a result of anything that he does to initiate or achieve salvation.

The fact is, a person who is not born again is spiritually dead in his trespasses—and dead things don't grow. The spiritually dead person cannot grow spiritually, and he cannot experience genuine intimacy with God, no matter how much "spirituality" he may claim to have or how much "communion" he may profess to have with God.

Now, before a person is saved, he might grow in his understanding about who Jesus is, about what Jesus did for him on the Cross, about his need for salvation, or about how to receive God's forgiveness. But he does not "grow into" salvation. Salvation is experienced by an act of believing that Jesus is the Christ, the Only begotten Son of God, and by personally accepting what Jesus did on the Cross—shedding His blood for the remission of our own sins. Those who confess their sinful nature to God, believe in Jesus and in His sacrificial, atoning death, and receive God's forgiveness through Jesus Christ are born again.

The following question is crucial for you to answer before proceeding any farther into the study. If you have not been born again in your spirit, you cannot grow spiritually into an intimate relationship with God.

⇜ Have you received Christ Jesus as your Savior? If so, when and how?

 If you have not accepted Jesus as your Savior, what is preventing you from doing so right now?

In being born again, a person becomes spiritually alive. As Peter wrote, we are "born again, not of corruptible seed but incorruptible, through the word of God" (1 Pet. 1:23). Incorruptible seed is eternal and life-giving seed. It is seed that does not die, but continues to live and is expected to produce growth and fruit.

One of the marks of all living things in the natural world is growth. A baby is born, and if he is healthy and normal physically, that baby begins immediately to receive nourishment and grow. A baby who fails to grow is diagnosed with "failure to thrive"—a situation that can be deadly if it goes untreated. In the spiritual realm, a newborn believer is expected to grow and develop, to change and mature. A failure to thrive will not bring about spiritual death or a loss of one's salvation, but it can produce a spiritual "deadening" which can result in a great loss of joy and significantly falling short of that person's potential and purpose in Christ Jesus.

Growth toward maturity is to be the norm of the Christian experience. It is the reason that God gave the fivefold ministry to the church (Eph. 4:11–15). It is to be the desire of every believer.

And He Himself gave some to be apostles, some prophets, some evangelists, and some pastors and teachers, for the equipping of the saints for the work of ministry, for the edifying of the body of Christ, till we all come to the unity of the faith and of the knowledge of the Son of God, to a perfect man, to the measure of the stature of the fullness of Christ; that we should no longer be children, tossed to and fro and carried about with every wind of doctrine, by the trickery of men, in the cunning craftiness of deceitful plotting, but, speaking the truth in love, may grow up in all things into Him who is the head—Christ.

—Ephesians 4:11–15

&. What sort of "equipping" does a Christian need for effective "work of ministry"? How do the gifts listed (pastors, teachers, etc.) help believers to be better equipped?

&. What sorts of "growth" are described in these verses? How is such growth attained? In what sense can a person *not* "grow" into salvation?

Ten Signs of Spiritual Growth

There are ten means by which we can evaluate whether we are growing spiritually. These are the signs that appear in the lives of those who are maturing in Christ. These signs are not to be used in judging or evaluating other people—we are to evaluate ourselves spiritually, not others. Neither should we assume that all ten signs will appear at all times in all who are growing spiritually. These are ten ways of evaluating positive, healthy spiritual growth—of recognizing a pattern that leads to spiritual maturity. We will deal with four of these signs in this chapter, and six in the following chapter.

Sign 1: A Growing Hunger to Know God

Those who are growing spiritually have a hunger for God. They are not content with knowing Him in an objective way as "Creator," "Savior," or "almighty God." Rather, they desire to know Him as Lord—to know what the Lord desires for them, and to know the experience of the Lord's presence in their lives on a daily basis.

Furthermore, they want to know the fullness of God—Father, Son, and Holy Spirit. Their hunger to know God will extend to a hunger to recognize and respond to the presence of the Holy Spirit on a daily basis.

As the deer pants for the water brooks, so pants my soul for You, O God. My soul thirsts for God, for the living God. When shall I come and appear before God?

—Psalm 42:1, 2

When have you experienced a desperate physical thirst or hunger? What was it like? How did it affect your thoughts and motivations? What was it like to finally satisfy that need?

When have you experienced a similar need for God? How can such a longing for God's presence be deliberately cultivated, rather than waiting for some special circumstance?

Sign 2: A Desire to Know God's Truth

The spiritually maturing person will have an *increasing* desire to know the truth of God's Word. Knowing the truth of God's Word extends beyond knowing what the Bible has to say. It goes beyond knowing Bible stories, Bible commandments, or the words of Jesus. To know the truth means to know the meaning of the Scriptures and to be able apply them to daily situations and relationships.

Now, we must read God's Word to know God's Word and to be able to take in its truth. So many people, including Christians, read certain magazines and newspapers each day more than they read their Bibles. This is not to discount the value of magazines and newspapers, but rather to call attention to the fact that we think about what we read. What we read has the potential to influence our opinions, our emotions, and our behavior. Surely the Bible should be the top priority on a Christian's daily reading agenda—and it is the top priority for those who are seeking to grow spiritually and develop an intimate relationship with God.

The Word of God is the one sure thing that we can count on for truth. It is the one thing that lasts forever in its application to the human heart. There is no greater nourishment for the soul, no greater food that promotes spiritual growth.

I rise before the dawning of the morning, and cry for help;
I hope in Your word. My eyes are awake through the night
watches, that I may meditate on Your word.

—Psalm 119:147, 148

What things did the psalmist do in these verses to know God's Word more fully? What steps do you take to know His Word?

16

What does it mean to meditate on God's Word? How is this done? Why is it important?

Sign 3: A Greater Sensitivity to Sin and Evil

The person who is growing spiritually will have an increasing ability to discern evil and to recognize sin, and an increasing abhorrence for all that is evil and sinful. One of the names for the Holy Spirit is the Spirit of Truth. It is the Holy Spirit who sharpens our awareness of error and our ability to distinguish right from wrong. The Christian is called and enabled to develop a heightened discernment regarding what is pleasing to the Lord and what isn't.

Christians are called to judge right from wrong (see 1 Pet. 4:17). This does not mean that we are to judge people; rather, we are to judge the righteousness of our own actions and words. It is the Holy Spirit who gives us the ability to test spiritual matters to see if they are truly of God, including testing things that are taught or preached to us, to discern if they are in line with God's Word (see 1 John 4:1–3).

The person who is maturing spiritually and entering into a more intimate relationship with the Lord will have an increasing desire to shun evil and to remove himself as far as possible from activities and situations that give rise to sin.

For the time has come for judgment to begin at the house of God; and if it begins with us first, what will be the end of those who do not obey the gospel of God?

—1 Peter 4:17

☙ What sort of "judgment" is Peter referring to here? How is it done?

Beloved, do not believe every spirit, but test the spirits, whether they are of God; because many false prophets have gone out into the world. By this you know the Spirit of God: Every spirit that confesses that Jesus Christ has come in the flesh is of God, and every spirit that does not confess that Jesus Christ has come in the flesh is not of God. And this is the spirit of the Antichrist, which you have heard was coming, and is now already in the world.

—1 John 4:1–3

☙ What does it mean to "test the spirits" when you hear God's Word taught or preached? How is this done? Why is it important?

 How well are you doing at "judging" yourself according to God's Word? How well are you testing the spirits of teaching? Where might you need to improve?

Sign 4: A Decreasing Desire for the World's System

The Bible teaches very clearly that, although we as believers are *in* this world, we are not to be *of* this world. As believers *in* the world, we must abide by natural law and live within the constraints of man-made laws. We must work and relate to others and provide for ourselves within the systems of this world. But we are not *of* this world—we do not have the same desires and lusts that the world exhibits. We do not have the same dreams, goals, or hopes that sinners have. We desire the things of God, not the things that fulfill the "lust of the flesh, the lust of the eyes, and the pride of life" (1 John 2:16).

I once knew a man who enjoyed going shopping with his wife each weekend. They often traveled a hundred miles or more on a Saturday to shop in nearby cities. One day they said to me, "Since we came to Christ and began to grow in Him, we find that we have far less desire to spend our money on those things that are temporary. Instead, we find ourselves talking more and more about supporting those things that bear eternal fruit." This man and his wife were maturing in the Lord!

The more you grow up spiritually, the less desire you will have for material things and the greater your desire will be to invest and participate in those things that have the potential to win souls and bear eternal fruit. Jesus taught, "Do not lay up for yourselves treasures on earth, where moth and rust destroy and where thieves break in and steal; but lay up for yourselves treasures in heaven, where neither moth nor rust destroys and where thieves do not break in and steal. For where your treasure is, there your heart will be also" (Matt. 6:19–21).

The person who is growing spiritually is far more concerned with pleasing God than pleasing men. The opinions of others have little effect on the spiritually mature person; he cares increasingly, however, about what is pleasing to God.

What "treasures on earth" have you laid up in your life? What "treasures in heaven" are you presently laying up?

In what areas of your life this week might you need to adjust your priorities, from earthly treasure to eternal treasure? How will you do this?

Today and Tomorrow

TODAY: AS I GROW IN CHRIST, MY PRIORITIES WILL BECOME MORE LIKE GOD'S PRIORITIES.

TOMORROW: I WILL SPEND TIME THIS WEEK EVALUATING WHERE MY TREASURE LIES, AND WILL FOCUS MORE ON ETERNAL GAIN.

Are You Growing? (Part 2)

───────── ❧ In This Lesson ❧ ─────────

LEARNING: WHAT ROLE DOES LOVE PLAY IN THE PROCESS OF GROWTH?

GROWING: WHY DOES JESUS COMMAND ME TO LOVE THE UNLOVABLE, FOR-
GIVE THE UNFORGIVEABLE?

───────── ∞ ─────────

Every Christian is called to submit daily to the indwelling presence of the Holy Spirit, to seek continuously to be conformed to the likeness of Jesus Christ, and to mature in his faith. Change for the better is to be the pattern of the Christian life—God is never content with the status quo of our character development, our witness, our reliance upon Him, or the depth of our relationship with Him. He wants us each to draw near to Him—and nearer still—so that He might impart to us the fullness of His presence and His blessings.

In the last lesson, we took a look at fours signs of spiritual growth. In this lesson, we will take a look at six additional means of evaluating our own spiritual growth.

Sign 5: An Increasing Sphere of Love

The person who is growing in Christ will have an ever-increasing ability to love others. As that love increases, it spreads out to an ever-widening circle of people. The maturing Christian can often look back and say,

"I never would have thought that I could reach out to that person with Christ's love." As we mature in Christ, our concern with appearances, status, and personal reputation decreases. Our concern with expressing God's love to the sinner and to the person in need increases.

We find that we are able to forgive people that we once thought unforgiveable, because we have grown in our understanding that, apart from the grace of God, we would be in the same unforgiven state. We find that we are able to give freely to people without attempts at manipulation, because we have grown in our understanding that we are to give freely what has been given to us: God's mercy and long-suffering kindness. We find that we are able to love without placing conditions on our love. We are able to say, "I love you" without adding "if you" or "when you" or "unless you" statements, because we recognize that God's love for us is unconditional.

Furthermore, the maturing Christian finds that he is more willing to express love to others—to reach out, to touch, to speak, to share, to listen, to be present in times of need. The person who is growing in Christ has an increasing desire to be used by God to shower His love on others.

If someone says, "I love God," and hates his brother, he is a liar; for he who does not love his brother whom he has seen, how can he love God whom he has not seen? And this commandment we have from Him: that he who loves God must love his brother also.

—1 John 4:20, 21

23

🕊 Without naming names, who do you have a difficult time loving? Why? How do these verses apply to that relationship?

🕊 What does it mean to love your brother? How is this done in practical, day-to-day terms?

Sign 6: A Quickness to Forgive Others

The spiritually maturing person finds it easier and easier to forgive those who have wronged him, hurt him, or rejected him. He is more sensitive to the need to forgive those who offend, and he is quicker to make apologies, to make amends, and to bring quarrels or disputes to a peaceful resolution. This does not mean that the spiritually mature person compromises with evil. Nor does it mean that the maturing Christian has a greater desire to be yoked with nonbelievers. Far from it! It does mean that the growing Christian has a desire to live in peace with others, not holding grudges or harboring resentment and bitterness.

When we fail to forgive, we remain tied to a person. To forgive is to set another person free from the binding grip of our heart and to entrust that person to God's care, love, and judgment. It is to let go of all desire for revenge or retribution, and to trust God to work in another person's life according to His plan and purposes.

> For if you forgive men their trespasses, your heavenly Father will also forgive you. But if you do not forgive men their trespasses, neither will your Father forgive your trespasses.
>
> —Matthew 6:14, 15

✎ A Christian can never lose his or her salvation, so in what sense will the Father not forgive your sins if you don't forgive others?

25

🕭 Why does God place such importance on forgiving others? Why is it such a priority in God's kingdom for His children to be forgiving of one another?

Sign 7: An Increasing Desire to Obey God

The person who is growing spiritually will have an ever-increasing desire to keep God's commandments and to obey the voice of the Holy Spirit, regardless of circumstances or what others around him are doing. The person who is becoming spiritually mature is less and less influenced by the will of others. He has a growing desire to know all of God's commandments and to live according to them.

God's commandments for our lives are not limited to the Ten Commandments or to the laws that we find in the Old Testament. They are not even limited to the commandments of Jesus that we find throughout the Gospels and in the Sermon on the Mount (see Matt. 5–7). They include the commands that the Lord gives to us by His Holy Spirit on a daily basis—commands to "go here," "do this," "say this," and "give that."

The mature Christian wants to do God's will. His answer is always yes to God's leading. The more a Christian matures, and the more intimate a relationship the person has with the Father, the quicker the person is to hear God's voice and to respond enthusiastically and with full effort to whatever God commands.

Therefore whoever hears these sayings of Mine, and does them, I will liken him to a wise man who built his house on the rock: and the rain descended, the floods came, and the winds blew and beat on that house; and it did not fall, for it was founded on the rock. But everyone who hears these sayings of Mine, and does not do them, will be like a foolish man who built his house on the sand: and the rain descended, the floods came, and the winds blew and beat on that house; and it fell. And great was its fall.

—Matthew 7:24–27

In what ways is obedience to God's Word similar to building on a firm foundation? How is this done, in practical terms?

When have you seen someone's plans collapse because they were built on some wrong ideas? How is this similar to knowing God's Word but not obeying it?

Sign 8: Ever-Increasing Faith

The person who is growing spiritually manifests greater and greater faith—an increased capacity to believe God and to trust Him to work in increasingly difficult circumstances. Many Christians believe that faith is static. They read Romans 12:3, "God has dealt to each one a measure of faith," and conclude that the faith which we receive inherently from God is a fixed entity. Jesus, however, spoke of varying degrees of faith. At one point, He chastised his disciples for having "little faith" (see Matt. 14:31). In another incident, He said to a Canaanite woman who came seeking the healing of her daughter, "Great is your faith!" (Matt. 15:28).

Faith is to be exercised. Our faith is capable of growing and becoming stronger the more we use it. The more we trust God to meet our needs and to do those things that only God can do in our lives, the more we see God at work in our lives. And the more God does in us and through us, the more evidence we have of God's presence and power—and the more we are willing to trust Him with even more of our lives. Our faith expands the more we trust God and rely upon Him to act in His sovereign way, according to His sovereign timing, and always for His sovereign purposes. If you are not using your faith to trust God for things that seem impossible, then your faith is not growing.

Sign 9: An Increasing Concern for Others

The person who is growing spiritually will have an ever-increasing concern for the welfare of others, and especially for the spiritual condition of others. He will have a strong desire to see sinners receive Jesus Christ as their Savior. He will have a desire to see the practical and emotional needs of others met. The maturing Christian will have an increasingly soft heart—a tender heart that is sensitive to others and quick to respond in whatever ways are appropriate and possible in meeting needs in others.

We should never forget that Jesus wept over Jerusalem, saying, "If you had known, even you, especially in this your day, the things that make for your peace! But now they are hidden from your eyes. For days will come upon you when your enemies will build an embankment around you, surround you and close you in on every side, and level you, and your children within you, to the ground; and they will not leave in you one stone upon another, because you did not know the time of your visitation" (Luke 19:42–44). Jesus wept at the tomb of his friend Lazarus (see John 11:35). We, too, are called to weep with those who weep and to rejoice with those who rejoice (see Rom. 12:15).

ᴥ When has someone wept because you were weeping? Rejoiced because you were rejoicing? How did these things influence you?

ᴥ Notice the stern words of judgment which Jesus used in the Luke 19 passage above. When does a concern for others call for stern discipline? How does one know whether gentleness or firmness is called for?

29

Sign 10: Love Toward God

The person who is growing spiritually is going to have increased love toward God. Many people feel resentment toward God from their early childhood, or perhaps as a result of something that happened to them as a teenager or young adult. They may have accepted the forgiveness of God by believing in Jesus Christ and His atoning death on the Cross, but they continue to distrust God or, for any number of reasons, desire a degree of distance from God.

The person who is maturing in Christ comes to recognize that God is our loving, merciful, tender, patient heavenly Father—and as such, He can be trusted completely to be our provider, counselor, source of all good blessings, and friend. The early misperceptions about God melt away the more a person comes to know God. And the clearer and more accurate a picture we have of God, the more we desire to be in His presence and know Him fully.

Jesus said that He came to show us the Father. He came to reveal the nature and character of the Father. When we look at Jesus, we see One who is infinitely approachable, ever-ready to meet the needs of those who come to Him with genuineness of heart, and One who loved to the degree of pouring out His life in sacrifice for others. To know Jesus is to love Jesus. To know Jesus is to know the Father. The more we know the Father, the more we love the father.

He who has My commandments and keeps them, it is he who loves Me. And he who loves Me will be loved by My Father, and I will love him and manifest Myself to him.

—John 14:21

30

How can you tell whether or not you truly love God, according to Jesus' words in these verses? Why did Jesus link obedience with true love?

In what sense is God's love "conditional" in these verses? In what sense is God's love *not* conditional? How can these concepts be reconciled without mutual contradiction?

Not all of these signs of spiritual growth may be evident in any one person at any given time. In general, however, a great majority of them are manifested by those who are maturing in Christ Jesus. Take a look again at the ten means of evaluation for spiritual growth that we have discussed in these last two lessons and check off those that you believe are true for you:

1. A growing hunger to know God
2. A desire to know God's truth
3. A greater sensitivity to sin and evil
4. A decreasing desire for the world's system
5. An increasing sphere of love
6. A quickness to forgive others
7. An increasing desire to obey God
8. Ever-increasing faith
9. An increasing concern for others
10. Feelings of love toward God

Which items in the above list need to be strengthened in your life? How will you strengthen them this week?

Today and Tomorrow

TODAY: HOW MUCH I LOVE GOD IS SHOWN BY HOW MUCH I LOVE OTHERS.

TOMORROW: I WILL SPEND TIME THIS WEEK IN SHOWING LOVE FOR SOMEONE WHO IS DIFFICULT TO LOVE.

Notes and Prayer Requests:

LESSON 4

Requirements for Growth Toward Intimacy with God (Part 1)

---------------- ❧ In This Lesson ☙ ----------------

LEARNING: HOW DOES INTIMACY WITH GOD GROW IN A PERSON'S LIFE?

GROWING: WHAT HAPPENS WHEN I FAIL?

☙

To a great extent, spiritual growth is a learning process, a learning that is rooted in the spirit, not in the mind—but nonetheless a learning process that is based upon acquisition of new knowledge and understanding, and the application of that knowledge in the context of our relationships with God and other people.

All of us know from our years in school that certain skills are considered to be prerequisite to other skills. For example, a child needs to learn his letters and numbers before he can read, spell, and do simple arithmetic. The same principle applies to spiritual growth.

There are seven things that are vital for growing in your Christian walk. These are necessary foundational principles, the essentials required of every person, regardless of age, culture, or denomination. We will discuss three of these prerequisites in this lesson and four in the next.

The Command to Grow

Peter said, "Grow in the grace and knowledge of our Lord and Savior Jesus Christ" (2 Pet. 3:18). This statement is in the imperative—it is a command to us—and therefore, we can conclude that spiritual growth is something that requires our human will. We do not automatically grow. We must choose to grow spiritually. We must pursue these seven requirements for spiritual growth with our full intention and will. Each of these seven essentials for spiritual growth should be approached with the understanding that we can do these things. The real questions are: Do we want to do them? Are we willing to make the effort to do them? Are we willing to make the changes in our lives that are required for spiritual growth?

Requirement 1: Renewal of the Mind

Any believer who desires to grow spiritually and move toward a more intimate relationship with God must choose to renew his mind. Whether you like it or not, you have been preprogrammed to think in certain ways from childhood. You have acquired certain belief systems, opinions, ideas, and perspectives based upon what your parents and other adults around you thought, said, and did. Some of the preprogramming that you received was very likely in contradiction to the Word of God, even if your parents were Christians and you were brought up in the church. No parent is perfect and, therefore, no childhood is perfect. We all have a degree of relearning to do—some of us more than others.

When the Israelites left Egypt, the Lord recognized that His people had been "Egyptianized" in their thinking and their approach toward life. They had lived as slaves in a land filled with false gods. Much of what the Israelites experienced in their forty years of wandering in the wilderness can be regarded as a "reshaping" of the Israelites' minds and hearts so that they might truly become the people of God, capable of taking authority over Canaan. In the wilderness, they became a people united under a new law (the commandments of God given to Moses) and new rituals related to their faith.

Just like the Israelites, we who are born again leave an alien land of sinfulness and are on a journey toward the fullness of God's promises and blessings in our lives. We must choose not to be shaped by the world's systems and images, but to be shaped by the Word of God. As we read in Romans 12:2, "Do not be conformed to this world, but be transformed by the renewing of your mind, that you may prove what is that good and acceptable and perfect will of God."

> I beseech you therefore, brethren, by the mercies of God, that you present your bodies a living sacrifice, holy, acceptable to God, which is your reasonable service. And do not be conformed to this world, but be transformed by the renewing of your mind, that you may prove what is that good and acceptable and perfect will of God.
>
> —Romans 12:1, 2

What does it mean to renew your mind? How is this done? What role does one's thinking have on the process of being "transformed"?

≈ What does it mean to "present your bodies a living sacrifice"?
What part does this play in the process of renewing one's mind?

Every gardener knows that it isn't enough for a person to pull up the
weeds in a garden. New plants must be planted in the soil that was
once occupied by the weeds for the garden to flourish and be productive and beautiful. Untended, unplanted soil will only produce more
weeds. In like manner, it isn't sufficient for us simply to be born again
in our spirit. We must begin to retrain our spirits and our minds to
respond to life as God wants us to respond. This means a great change
in various habits, procedures, thought processes, and belief systems.
We must renew our thinking, our speaking, and our behaving to line
up with our salvation.

How do we do this? By filling our minds with the Word of God. We
must read the Bible frequently—at least once a day—and sufficiently.
We will know that we have read the Bible sufficiently when we find
ourselves saying about a particular passage, "I see in this something
that I now must do or change in my life."

For the word of God is living and powerful, and sharper than any two-edged sword, piercing even to the division of soul and spirit, and of joints and marrow, and is a discerner of the thoughts and intents of the heart.

—Hebrews 4:12

What does this verse mean by "the division of soul and spirit"? Why is this an important process in spiritual growth? How does God's Word accomplish this?

When has God's Word addressed "the thoughts and intents" of your heart? What changes resulted from that experience?

Requirement 2: Readiness to Face Failures

Most of us try to sidestep or justify our failures and faults. We like to take the easy way out, saying, "That's just the way I am" or, "That's the way my parents raised me." The fact is, most of us are not just the way God wants us to be. In order to get from where we are to where God wants us to be, we have to make changes in our lives. And that means facing our faults and failures, taking responsibility for them, and going to God with them.

Is there an area in your life in which you have experienced repeated failures? Are you aware of certain faults that you have, and seem always to have had? Have you been trying for years to sidestep, outrun, or ignore those failures and faults in hopes that God will forget about them? Let me assure you today that God won't forget them. In His desire to see you made strong, God will continue to pursue those areas in your life that are weak. In His desire to see you made whole, He will continue to pursue those faults and failures that fragment you and cause you disharmony, dysfunction, or uneasiness. In His desire to draw you closer to Himself, God will continue to move against any barrier that stands in the way of His experiencing genuine spiritual intimacy with you.

The first step that each of us must take is to admit our failures, flaws, and faults. We must own up to our finiteness and our weaknesses. And we must assume responsibility for our failures. We must not blame others for what has happened to us, but confess to God, "I have brought myself to the place where I am today." Even though others may have wounded you, rejected you, or sinned against you, your response to their actions has made you who you are today. If you are to grow spiritually, you must own up to your actions and reactions.

If we say that we have no sin, we deceive ourselves, and the truth is not in us. If we confess our sins, He is faithful and just to forgive us our sins and to cleanse us from all unrighteousness. If we say that we have not sinned, we make Him a liar, and His word is not in us.

—1 John 1:8–10

🙢 Have you sinned? Do you still sometimes sin, even though you have been born again into Christ's redemption? Why does sin continue to occur in the lives of Christians?

🙢 What is the result of confessing that you still have sin in your life? How is this an important step to having *less* sin in the future?

Requirement 3: Repentance of Sin

To repent is to turn around, to move in the opposite direction, to make a complete about-face. Many people believe that we must repent before we can receive God's forgiveness. That is not what the Bible says. The Bible calls us to confess our sins, to own up to our sinful state, admit our need of a Savior, acknowledge our sin nature—and *receive* God's forgiveness for our sin. Then, enabled and empowered by the Holy Spirit dwelling within us, we are to repent: to change from our wicked ways, our evil attitudes, hurtful words, and wrong behaviors. No person is capable of true repentance apart from the power of the Holy Spirit working within. It is our will plus His power that gives us the willpower to make genuine changes in our lives. The person who desires to grow spiritually must be willing to change and to give up old sinful habits, desires, lusts, thoughts, and associations.

In 1 Peter 2:1, we read this admonition: "Therefore [since this gospel has been preached to you], laying aside all malice, all deceit, hypocrisy, envy, and all evil speaking. . . ." Peter tells the young believers to lay aside or to "put off" these behaviors. The literal Greek word means to "strip away," as one strips away garments that are tattered and filthy. The believers are told to strip away malice (wicked ill will); guile or deceit (deliberate dishonesty; hypocrisy); pretended piety and love; envy (resentful discontentment); and all manner of evil speaking, including slander, backbiting, and lying. Each of these behaviors is subject to the human will. The believers are to repent of these behaviors and to change their ways!

The New Testament has a number of similar passages in which believers are admonished to put off or stop one type of behavior, and in its place institute a righteous behavior. Always, these admonitions are given with the understanding that we are capable of doing this according to the power of the Holy Spirit working in us. The changes are not automatic, however. We must want to make them and work daily to make them.

Therefore we also, since we are surrounded by so great a cloud of witnesses, let us lay aside every weight, and the sin which so easily ensnares us, and let us run with endurance the race that is set before us, looking unto Jesus, the author and finisher of our faith, who for the joy that was set before Him endured the cross, despising the shame, and has sat down at the right hand of the throne of God.

—Hebrews 12:1, 2

What sins have ensnared you in the past week? What sort of "weight" might the Lord be calling you to lay aside this week?

How is endurance required in running a race? In what ways is this a good analogy for the process of purifying one's life of sinful behaviors?

One of the things that we must never lose sight of as we grow in our relationship with the Lord is that we love and worship a *Holy* God. God manifests no darkness, no shadow of turning, no tolerance for evil or deceit. For us to approach God, we must be in a state or forgiveness, which is only made possible as we trust Jesus Christ to be our Savior, Redeemer, Mediator, and Lord. Christ is our forgiveness and our righteousness.

The renewal of the mind, a confession of faults and sins, and repentance of sinful attitudes and behaviors are part of living in a state of righteousness. They are essential to our drawing close to a Holy God.

A person who willfully chooses to pursue the world's systems and who adopts the world's beliefs cannot draw close to God. His thinking and believing are in a direction totally opposite that of the Lord. A person who refuses to acknowledge sin and be forgiven of it cannot draw close to God. His sin continues to be a barrier to intimacy with the Lord. A person who refuses to repent of sinful attitudes and behaviors cannot draw close to God. His rebellion keeps from him from intimacy with a Holy God.

Do you desire today to grow spiritually? Then you must actively choose with your will to address your own sinfulness, choose to change your believing and behavior to line up with God's Word, and choose to wash your mind with the Word of God so that you might be cleansed and renewed in your thinking.

> Put off, concerning your former conduct, the old man which grows corrupt according to the deceitful lusts, and be renewed in the spirit of your mind, and . . . put on the new man which was created according to God, in true righteousness and holiness.

> —Ephesians 4:22–24

What was Paul referring to here as the "the old man"? How does one put it off? What is the "new man" that we must put on?

In what ways are lusts deceitful? In what ways does lust tend to deceive a person away from God's truth? What is the solution to this?

Today and Tomorrow

TODAY: MY VIEW OF SIN MUST BE THE SAME AS GOD'S VIEW IF I AM TO GROW IN INTIMACY WITH HIM.

TOMORROW: I WILL SPEND TIME THIS WEEK RENEWING MY MIND SO THAT I CAN BECOME TRANSFORMED IN CHRIST.

LESSON 5

Requirements for Growth Toward Intimacy with God (Part 2)

❧ In This Lesson ❧

LEARNING: WHO CAN HELP ME LEARN MORE ABOUT GOD?

GROWING: WHAT SHOULD I DO WHEN SUFFERING COMES?

In the last lesson, we covered three prerequisites for spiritual growth. In this lesson, we will deal with four additional essentials for a person to grow in Christ. These are things that God desires for us and which He enables us to do by the power of the Holy Spirit working in us. These are also things that require our will and effort. We must choose to grow spiritually and to draw close to God.

Requirement 4: Receive Godly Counsel

Every Christian, no matter the state of his spiritual maturity, should have a wise Christian friend with whom he can share his struggles, faults, failures, and spiritual hopes. Ideally, this friend will be a more spiritually mature believer who can serve as a mentor in the faith. If you do not have such a person in your life, I strongly encourage you to seek one out.

45

We must be open to receiving wise counsel, which is counsel couched in love, forgiveness, and confidentiality. We can learn a great deal from our brothers and sisters in Christ. As we listen to their experiences, we learn how God's Word can be applied in a wide variety of situations. We also can benefit greatly from their insights into the truth of God's Word and from their advice regarding our unique God-given plan and purpose in life. None of us is called to be a "lone ranger" in the faith. We are called to relate to one another as a *body* of believers that functions as a family. We are to be interdependent on one another in areas including the sharing of wisdom and knowledge.

In order to benefit from and to give wise counsel, we must choose to be transparent in our own lives and be vulnerable emotionally in the presence of others. We must be candid, forthcoming, and truthful in all that we say and do. The person who does not seek out the wise counsel of others is limited to his own perspective, deductions, reasoning ability, and information. And that, my friend, is a great limitation no matter how brilliant a person may be!

A wise man will hear and increase learning, and a man of understanding will attain wise counsel. . . The fear of the LORD is the beginning of knowledge, but fools despise wisdom and instruction. . . The way of a fool is right in his own eyes, but he who heeds counsel is wise.

—Proverbs 1:5, 7; 12:15

⋙ What roles does counsel play in attaining wisdom, according to these verses? What is required of a person who wants to attain wisdom?

⋙ What sort of person would make a good counselor, judging from these verses?

We never outgrow our need for wise counsel, no matter how spiritually mature we may be. Do not limit yourself to one area of counsel. Get God's wisdom in all areas of your life. Some people need wise counsel in how to be better stewards of their resources, others need wise counsel in how to grow in their prayer life, still others need wise counsel regarding marital or family problems. God's wisdom extends to every area of human existence. You can never receive enough wisdom. If believers around you are not able to give you wise counsel, go to other sources—perhaps to godly men and women in professional fields or to books or tapes produced by strong Christians. Much of the wisdom of the Christian church through the ages is available to you in books, commentaries, Bible teaching tapes, and other media.

And finally, ask God for His wisdom. Ask the Holy Spirit to be your Counselor, your guide into all spiritual truth. Jesus promised His disciples that He would send them the "Spirit of truth who proceeds from the Father, He will testify of Me" (John 15:26). The Holy Spirit is given to us to "convict the world of sin, and of righteousness, and of judgment" (see John 16:8)—in other words, to enable us to discern at all times good from evil and righteousness from unrighteousness.

> If any of you lacks wisdom, let him ask of God, who gives to all liberally and without reproach, and it will be given to him. But let him ask in faith, with no doubting, for he who doubts is like a wave of the sea driven and tossed by the wind. For let not that man suppose that he will receive anything from the Lord; he is a double-minded man, unstable in all his ways.

> —James 1:5–8

Why does doubt make a person "unstable in all his ways"? What does it mean to be double-minded? How can doubt make a person try to obey two conflicting agendas?

↞ Why does God withhold wisdom from doubters? Why is faith a prerequisite for gaining wisdom?

Requirement 5: Service to Others

We do not learn in isolation, nor do we grow spiritually in isolation. We learn and grow in relationship to others. Many people attend church Sunday after Sunday without any apparent change in their lives. Church is just something that they do on Sunday mornings before they go out to eat. That is not God's desire!

God desires that we attend church so that we might learn more about the Lord and His commandments, worship the Lord with others, pray for our needs, and be inspired to continue steadfastly in the faith. We are then to leave the church each Sunday and seek as many ways as possible to apply what we have learned and to tell others what we have experienced in Christ Jesus.

All of us are to be servants to others in the faith. We are to minister to the needs of others and to love others. To be of service to others and to love others, we first must be in relationship with others. It is as we love and serve others that we discover more about our own spiritual nature and how to live the Christian life effectively and meaningfully. It is as we serve others, both believers and nonbelievers, that we learn more about our own weaknesses and Christ's strengths. The more we learn about Christ's strengths and His love, the more we grow in appreciation of the Lord, and the greater our desire to draw close to Him. What we learn through service is absolutely vital to our spiritual growth.

> For you, brethren, have been called to liberty; only do not use liberty as an opportunity for the flesh, but through love serve one another. For all the law is fulfilled in one word, even in this: *"You shall love your neighbor as yourself."*
>
> —Galatians 5:13, 14

In what ways do Christians sometimes use their liberty to satisfy their flesh? What is the correct use of liberty, according to these verses?

How does learning to love your neighbor contradict the world's teachings concerning self-love and self-esteem? What does this command assume concerning one's love for oneself?

Requirement 6: Active Reflection About God's Work

A number of years ago, I became acquainted with the writings of an English preacher who died in 1917. I read one book that had been compiled by his wife and was greatly blessed by it. Through the years, I purchased all the available books of his teachings. Even today, Oswald Chambers is a great inspiration to me. I cannot begin to count the number of times that I have read *My Utmost for His Highest.*

The biographies of great Christians through the ages are worthy of our reading and reflection. Their life stories allow us to experience vicariously what they have suffered, learned, and accomplished by faith. It is as we learn about the ways in which God has worked in the lives of others that we gain an understanding about how God will work in our lives—not only the people that we read about in the Bible, but also believers in the course of history. We can also learn a great deal, of course, by hearing and reflecting upon the ways in which God is working in the lives of other Christians today.

As a boy, I spent four very meaningful days with my grandfather. He was a godly man, a preacher, and I learned much of what I know about trusting God from him as he told me stories of his own experiences in trusting God. Draw your children's attention to godly character traits in others. Give them patterns to follow as they develop godly traits in their own lives. Actively reflect upon what God is doing, and how He is accomplishing His purposes in those who trust in Him. You will learn a great deal, but more important, you will be inspired to grow spiritually and to seek a deeper relationship with your heavenly Father.

A disciple is not above his teacher, but everyone who is perfectly trained will be like his teacher.

—Luke 6:40

∽ What did Jesus mean when He said that "a disciple is not above his teacher"? What spirit is necessary in a disciple if he is to learn to be like his Master?

∽ Who do you know that reminds you of Christ? What things in that person's life make you think of Christ? How can you learn from that person's example?

Requirement 7: Responding to Trials

The person who desires to grow spiritually must recognize that every trial and test in life is an opportunity for spiritual learning. So many people believe that, when something bad happens to them, the devil caused it to happen. In most cases, the devil had nothing to do with it. The bad consequence is the result of a person's failure or another person's persecution. The fact is, God knows about all of the trials and tests that we face in life, and He has allowed them to come into our lives for a purpose. Trials and tests are our opportunity to learn more about God's methods, purposes, and perfect plan. They are our opportunities to become strengthened in faith and to prove ourselves worthy of an increased sphere of influence.

If you are to grow spiritually, you must choose not to run from trials and tests, nor to deny their existence. Instead, choose to focus on the Lord as you face a trial. Ask the Lord why He has allowed this in your life. Look for the lesson that He desires to teach you or the character trait that He wants to develop or strengthen. It is in our trials that the Lord reveals to us His great mercy, strength, and power—which are more than sufficient for any need we face.

God has a way of using every trial, failure, and setback for our eternal benefit. Look for the ways in which He wants to work in you to bear lasting spiritual fruit. If we run from trials, we will miss the great lessons that we can learn from our trials under the tutelage of the Holy Spirit.

A significant part of learning occurs when a person has a wise teacher, applies what he learns in active obedience, avails himself of the opportunity to learn vicariously from the mistakes and triumphs of others, and sees life lessons rising from his own hardships and trials. This is true in learning with the mind, and it is also true in those things that we learn with the heart. Choose to learn all that you can about why and how God works, and you will begin to grow spiritually and to develop an intimate relationship with the Lord.

> In this you greatly rejoice, though now for a little while, if need be, you have been grieved by various trials, that the genuineness of your faith, being much more precious than gold that perishes, though it is tested by fire, may be found to praise, honor, and glory at the revelation of Jesus Christ.
>
> —1 Peter 1:6, 7

In what ways can trials be like the process of purifying gold?

In what was Peter encouraging his audience to rejoice while they were suffering? What is required for a person to rejoice sincerely during hardship?

Today and Tomorrow

TODAY: I CAN LEARN A GREAT DEAL FROM THE WISDOM OF GODLY MEN AND WOMEN.

TOMORROW: I WILL SPEND TIME THIS WEEK BOTH SERVING OTHERS AND LEARNING FROM OTHERS.

LESSON 6

Stages of Growth Toward Intimacy (Part 1)

❧ In This Lesson ☙

LEARNING: HOW CAN I HOPE TO MEASURE WHETHER OR NOT I'M GROWING IN MY WALK WITH GOD?

GROWING: WHAT DO I DO WHEN I GET STUCK?

As a Christian matures spiritually, there are several stages that he goes through as he moves toward an intimate, personal relationship with the heavenly Father. These stages are a normal part of the growth process, a natural maturation process. Just as a healthy baby is born physically with all of the *potential* to develop various adult skills and traits, we are each born spiritually with the potential for great spiritual growth, maturity, and an intimate relationship with the Lord. Not all people choose to develop all of the physical, intellectual, or emotional gifts that they have been given. In like manner, not all believers choose to develop all the spiritual potential that they have been given. We must choose to develop our spiritual lives, just as we must choose to develop our God-given talents and abilities.

There are four things that I want to caution you about as you do this lesson: First, these stages in spiritual growth are not always clear-cut to us. At times, others close to us can see these stages in our lives more clearly than we see them. Ask the Holy Spirit to reveal to you where you are as you study these stages.

Second, these stages are not for comparative purposes. They are solely for you to use in gaining a better understanding of your level of spiritual maturity, as well as a better understanding of what the Lord may presently be doing in your life.

Third, you can get stuck in a phase if you are unwilling to move forward in your spiritual growth. No person can put a stop to your spiritual growth except you. God will not, and others cannot. You must choose not to be discouraged or to turn away from the Lord; rather, you must choose to push forward in your desire to know God and to become all that He wants you to be spiritually.

෴ When have you felt "stuck" in your spiritual life, as if you weren't growing and didn't know why? What did you do? What was the result?

෴ Have you ever felt like giving up on your walk with God? What did you do? What was the result?

Fourth, God is the One who is at work continually to move us from stage to stage. We cannot will ourselves into a new stage. These stages are His work, not ours. At the same time, there are certain things that we can do in any given stage to prepare ourselves for the coming stages.

We should no longer be children, tossed to and fro and carried about with every wind of doctrine, by the trickery of men, in the cunning craftiness of deceitful plotting, but, speaking the truth in love, may grow up in all things into Him who is the head—Christ—from whom the whole body, joined and knit together by what every joint supplies, according to the effective working by which every part does its share, causes growth of the body for the edifying of itself in love.

—Ephesians 4:14–16

In what ways are children likely to be "carried about" with every new thing they learn? How is this sometimes seen in new Christians?

What is the solution to this trait of being "tossed to and fro" by false doctrines? How is it an essential part of becoming a mature believer?

Seven Stages of Growth

Stage 1: Unbelief

All of us begin in a stage of unbelief. There was a time in the life of each Christian in which he did not place his trust in God, had no desire to know or keep God's commandments, and was dominated and directed by his fleshly, sinful nature. As John wrote, "If we say that we have no sin, we deceive ourselves" (1 John 1:8).

> All we like sheep have gone astray; we have turned, every one, to his own way; and the LORD has laid on Him the iniquity of us all.
>
> —Isaiah 53:6

🐑 Have you ever watched a flock of sheep? If so, how did they behave? In what ways is this a picture of human nature?

🐑 In your own words, what does it mean that God has laid on Jesus the iniquity of us all?

Stage 2: Salvation

When we are in a stage of unbelief, the Holy Spirit is nonetheless at work in our lives convicting us of our sinful nature and leading us to Jesus Christ so that we might receive the forgiveness that God makes available through the shed blood of His Son. Our spiritual life truly begins when we accept Jesus as our Savior and receive God's forgiveness and His free gift of the Holy Spirit into our lives.

Believing and receiving are active steps on our part. They require an action of our will. We choose to confess to the Father that we are sinners. We choose to believe that what Jesus did on the Cross provides the atonement for our sins and reconciles us to God. We choose to accept God's forgiveness and we choose to receive His Holy Spirit.

Most people who experience God's forgiveness—which we call "salvation" or being "born again"—have feelings of joy and peace. They feel clean inside. With salvation also comes a desire to know God, to know what the Bible says, and to share with others what God has done in giving them a new life.

> "Come now, and let us reason together," Says the LORD, "Though your sins are like scarlet, they shall be as white as snow; though they are red like crimson, they shall be as wool."
>
> —Isaiah 1:18

🐚 Have you ever tried to remove a stain from a white garment? What was it like? How is this a picture of sin?

᷒ Why did God say, "Let us reason together"? What part does one's reason play in the process of salvation?

Stage 3: Service

Those who are born again have an inevitable desire to serve the Lord in some way. Part of this desire is born of thanksgiving for their salvation; part of it is born of love for God; part of it is born of a desire to share with those whom we love the great joy, peace, and assurance about eternity that we have experienced.

Most Christians are properly taught that their service bears fruit and eternal reward (although our acts of service do *not* earn our salvation). Every person has a built-in desire to be of use and to have a purposeful existence. For the Christian, this desire finds its expression in loving service to others, including an active witness about Jesus Christ as Savior.

How has the Lord led you into service to others since you were born again? How has the service of others influenced your life?

But now we have been delivered from the law, having died to what we were held by, so that we should serve in the newness of the Spirit and not in the oldness of the letter.

—Romans 7:6

What does it mean to serve others "in the oldness of" the law? How can service be done with a grudging spirit of obligation? How is it different when done willingly and cheerfully?

Stage 4: Frustrated Inadequacy

As we serve the Lord to the best of our ability, we come to a place in our service where we realize that our motives are not always pure and our efforts are not always adequate. The result is a frustration at our inadequacy. This frustration can turn to discouragement if we do not come quickly to the truth of God's Word: By yourself, you cannot accomplish anything of eternal value; but with God, you can accomplish all things and produce eternal fruit.

Our feelings of frustration are not only experienced as we serve others. We also may experience feelings of frustration that our prayers aren't powerful enough, our motives aren't pure enough, our attitudes aren't right, our words are ineffective, our praise is hollow, our souls are empty. We come face-to-face with the fact that, although we are trying as hard as we can, we are not succeeding in the things that matter most to us.

Paul was the first to admit this stage of frustrated inadequacy. He wrote to the Romans:

For I know that in me (that is, in my flesh) nothing good dwells; for to will is present with me, but how to perform what is good I do not find. For the good that I will to do, I do not do; but the evil I will not to do, that I practice. . . O wretched man that I am! Who will deliver me from this body of death? I thank God—through Jesus Christ our Lord!

—Romans 7:18,19, 24, 25

62

🔖 When have you felt like Paul? What good things did you want to do? What evil things transpired instead?

🔖 When have you seen God's power in your life, bringing His own good things out of your inadequate service?

The good news to which we must cling when we experience this stage in our spiritual growth is this: In Christ we are adequate. There is no condemnation to those who are in Christ Jesus (see Rom. 8:1). He is our sufficiency, and in Him, we can do all things that He wants us to accomplish. We must continue to live and move and have our being in Him.

Stage 5: Spiritual Dependency

If we will press forward in our faith and continue to trust God even though we feel frustrated and inadequate, the Lord will bring us to a place where we can relax in total spiritual dependency upon Him. When we reach the end of our own ability and effort, we find that God is able to work in us and through us in ways that we never thought possible. We find that, as we become totally dependent upon the Holy Spirit for daily guidance, direction, and encouragement, our spiritual walk is more enjoyable and our work is more effective.

At this stage of our growth, we are actively choosing to be filled with the Holy Spirit on a daily basis. Now, the Holy Spirit indwells us at the point of our salvation, but a daily awareness of His presence and a "filling up" of His presence to cover our own recognized lack and inability is something that we must request of the Lord and receive from Him. It is an act of our will. The daily prayer for each of us must be, "Fill me, Lord, with Your presence. Use me. Work through me. May my will be totally and completely submitted to Your will so that Your will is done on this earth today, through me."

Not that we are sufficient of ourselves to think of anything as being from ourselves, but our sufficiency is from God, who also made us sufficient as ministers of the new covenant, not of the letter but of the Spirit; for the letter kills, but the Spirit gives life.

—2 Corinthians 3:5, 6

What "letter" is Paul speaking of in these verses? How does it kill one's ministry?

In what ways can a spirit of compulsion lead a person into frustration in ministry? How does the Holy Spirit breathe new life into one's attitude and service?

Today and Tomorrow

TODAY: I MUST REMEMBER THAT I AM UTTERLY DEPENDENT UPON GOD FOR ALL AREAS OF MY LIFE.

TOMORROW: I WILL ASK THE LORD TO BREATHE NEW LIFE INTO MY ATTITUDE AND MINISTRY THIS WEEK THROUGH THE POWER OF HIS HOLY SPIRIT.

Notes and Prayer Requests:

Stages of Growth Toward Intimacy (Part 2)

❧ In This Lesson ❧

LEARNING: WHAT PART DOES MY PAST PLAY IN MY PRESENT AND MY FUTURE?

GROWING: HOW CAN I GROW TO BE MORE LIKE CHRIST?

No person is automatically spiritually mature at the time he is born again. Just as in natural birth and growth, a new believer must mature in his walk with the Lord. This growth follows a normal pattern and occurs in stages over time. Unlike the physical maturation process, however, there is no accurate predictor of how much time a person may spend in any one stage of spiritual growth. It is the Lord who moves us from stage to stage. Our part is to make the right responses as each stage emerges and develops.

In the last lesson, we covered the first five of seven stages toward an intimate, personal relationship with the Lord. In review, these stages are:

1. Unbelief
2. Salvation
3. Service
4. Frustrated Inadequacy
5. Spiritual Dependency

In this lesson, we will continue our discussion with the last two stages of spiritual growth.

Stage 6: "The Battle"

A battle erupts in the life of every person who has reached a place of dependency upon the Holy Spirit. I call this the "Battle of Preprogrammed Bondage." It is a period of increasingly intense restlessness and discontentment in one's emotions. The believer knows without doubt that he is dependent upon the Holy Spirit for all effectiveness in ministry and for all joy in living, but at the same time, an inner conflict begins to develop. Questions begin to emerge about one's identity and one's emotional makeup. Many believers find themselves asking for the first time, in all seriousness, "Who am I? Why am I here?" A search emerges for purpose, meaning, and an understanding of one's uniqueness.

≈ Have you ever experienced this struggle in your own life? What questions or conflicts did you wrestle with?

≈ Are you still wrestling with these issues, or have you found some resolution? If so, what resolution did you come to? How did you arrive at that peace?

68

Many Christians who enter this stage in their spiritual growth believe that the devil is after them—they believe that they are under spiritual attack or that the devil is trying to oppress them or depress them into a return to their old sinful life. While this may be true in a few cases, in the vast majority of cases it is God who is directly causing this inner restlessness (and in all cases, it is God who is allowing it to occur).

What is God's purpose in this stage? That is the key question which we each must ask. The believer at this stage has already dealt with the sin issue of his life, and has come to a place of dependency upon the Holy Spirit. What the believer must now confront is the fact that our sin nature is changed when we are born again, but our emotions and our minds still need to undergo a transformation process.

A person can be born again, serve God, and come through a time of frustration that ends in total dependency upon the Holy Spirit, and still never deal with emotional and mental patterns—ways of thinking, rationalizing, believing, and responding to life—that are carried over from the old life. Most of us carry these old patterns with us long into our Christian walk. They are the products of bad teaching, bad examples, rejection, and often of abusive experiences and conditional love. These patterns are like old recordings that play inside us—they manifest themselves in habits, rituals, and behaviors that are not in keeping with God's desire for us. And it is up to us, in this time of God-produced restlessness and discontentment, to confront these patterns head-on. God brings us to this point so that we might deal with the early lies, deceit, and hurts that we have experienced and that keep us from moving fully into an intimate relationship with Him.

❧ Can you cite examples of old emotional patterns or old attitudes that affect you spiritually? Things that are in conflict with God's truth?

❧ When have you experienced bad teaching, bad examples, abuse, rejection, or conditional love? Have you found healing of these old wounds, or do they still influence you in some way?

This "Battle of Preprogrammed Bondage" lies entirely within us, although it may manifest itself in bouts of anger (even rage), frustration, depression, and withdrawal from others. The challenge that we face is to discover what Christ wants us to know about ourselves. It is a time for us to confront our past and our inner makeup and to experience God's healing for those areas that lie wounded and scarred deep within.

Why does the Lord wait until we are in this stage of our spiritual life to deal with these things? Probably because to do so earlier would completely devastate us. It seems that a person needs to have a deep assurance of his salvation and his relationship to the Holy Spirit before he can truly trust God to be the healer of his entire being. Any living plant needs to develop roots and reach a healthy size before it is pruned, shaped, or grafted. So, too, with us as believers. Those who have been freed from sin and sealed forever by the Holy Spirit need a time to grow and become established in the Lord before the Lord begins to prune away those things that keep us from wholeness.

What we need to keep in mind is that this stage is designed by God for our healing and wholeness as human beings. God desires to restore, replenish, and renew in us things that have been broken, damaged, or stunted.

> Therefore we do not lose heart. Even though our outward man is perishing, yet the inward man is being renewed day by day. For our light affliction, which is but for a moment, is working for us a far more exceeding and eternal weight of glory, while we do not look at the things which are seen, but at the things which are not seen. For the things which are seen are temporary, but the things which are not seen are eternal.
>
> —2 Corinthians 4:16–18

≈ List below the reasons that Paul gave in these verses for not losing heart during this spiritual battle.

≈ What is the "far more exceeding and eternal weight of glory"? What "things which are seen" are you wrestling with? What "things which are not seen" is the Lord working on?

I suggest that you take these three very positive steps as you face the "Battle of Preprogrammed Bondage":

First, pray earnestly that the Lord will reveal to you all areas of bondage that are limiting you in your emotions and mind. Ask Him to reveal those areas where He wants you to confront your life and make changes or seek healing. Second, ask the Lord to reveal to you where you might go to receive help or to whom you might go for wise counseling or prayer. Third, as the Lord reveals various wounds from your past, burrow into God's Word and seek out the fullness of God's answer of healing to those hurts. And then receive by your faith the healing that the Lord offers to you. He makes available to you His presence, mercy, forgiveness, and love—He desires that you be whole in spirit, mind, and body.

There are those who do not have a great deal of bad preprogramming from their childhoods. There are also those who have benefited from good Christian counseling earlier in their Christian walk. These individuals may not experience as intense a battle at this stage of their spiritual growth. Nonetheless, we all face a battle that involves some degree of spiritual error that we have taken into our lives.

The work of the Lord in this stage of our spiritual life is ongoing. The more the Lord reveals to us about ourselves, the more we recognize that we need His healing presence within us, active at all times, to make us whole. The more we acknowledge that the healing work is His, the more we can relax in His presence and yield to the lessons that He desires to teach us, even those lessons that may be initially painful or uncomfortable.

Do not lie to one another, since you have put off the old man with his deeds, and have put on the new man who is renewed in knowledge according to the image of Him who created him.

—Colossians 3:9, 10

What does it mean to "put off the old man"? How is this done? How does this spiritual battle figure into that process?

What does it mean to be "renewed in knowledge"? How is this done? How does this spiritual battle figure into that process?

Stage 7: The Exchanged Life

In the final stage of our spiritual growth, we recognize that the Holy Spirit does not indwell us simply to help us or heal us, but to live Christ's life through us in order to touch others. It is in this stage that we come to believe with our heart and to embody in our whole life the truth that Christ dwells within us and that the life which we live is no longer our own, but His. Everything is yielded to Him. We no longer have goals or desires that are exclusively our own; rather, our goals and desires flow from what He desires and has planned on our behalf. The sole purpose of our lives is to know Christ and to be His instrument of righteousness in this world. Our heart's desire is to be used by Him for His eternal purposes.

In this final stage of our spiritual growth, we have a deep hunger for the Lord. We desire to spend more time with Him, to know Him more intimately, and to enter into long periods of prayer and study of the Scriptures so that we might hear His voice more clearly and know His heart more fully. Nothing gives us as much joy as spending time with the Lord. Nothing energizes us as much as hearing a direction or a word of encouragement from the Lord. We live to praise and serve the Lord in all that we say and do.

We do not grow out of this final stage of the exchanged life—"I in Christ and Christ in me." Rather, we mature in our understanding of what it means for Christ to live His life through us. We grow in our desire to be transformed fully into His likeness and to be one with Christ. Indeed, this is the life that we will experience for all eternity.

I have been crucified with Christ; it is no longer I who live, but Christ lives in me; and the life which I now live in the flesh I live by faith in the Son of God, who loved me and gave Himself for me.

—Galatians 2:20

In theological terms, what does it mean to be "crucified with Christ"? What does it mean in practical, day-to-day terms?

When have you experienced a life lived "by faith in the Son of God"? What brought you to that level of faith? How did it influence your attitudes and behaviors?

❧ Today and Tomorrow ❧

TODAY: WHEN ISSUES FROM MY PAST CROP UP, I WILL REMEMBER THAT GOD IS THE ONE DOING THE TRANSFORMING WORK IN MY LIFE— AND I WILL NOT LOSE HEART.

TOMORROW: I WILL ASK THE LORD TO HELP ME TO LIVE BY FAITH MORE AND MORE THIS WEEK.

❧ Notes and Prayer Requests: ❧

God's Formula for Spiritual Growth (Part 1)

―――――――― ❧ **In This Lesson** ☙ ――――――――

LEARNING: WHAT SHOULD I DO WITH THE THINGS I LEARN FROM GOD'S WORD?

GROWING: WHY CAN'T I REMEMBER WHAT I'VE LEARNED?

―――――― ☙⊗☙ ――――――

Most people are given advice when they are born again—it generally takes the form of things to *do* now that the person is a Christian. The advice usually includes the basics of Christian discipline: Attend church regularly, read the Bible daily, pray daily, give tithes and offerings regularly, and be faithful in service to others.

These disciplines are vital to the Christian life, but they are not a formula for spiritual growth. Rather, they are disciplines related to obeying God's commandments. For spiritual growth, God has a much different formula. We find evidence of it in James 1:21–25, which says:

> Therefore lay aside all filthiness and overflow of wickedness, and receive with meekness the implanted word, which is able to save your souls. But be doers of the word, and not hearers only, deceiving yourselves. For if anyone is a hearer of the word and not a doer, he is like a man observing his natural

face in a mirror; for he observes himself, goes away, and immediately forgets what kind of man he was. But he who looks
into the perfect law of liberty and continues in it, and is not a
forgetful hearer but a doer of the work, this one will be blessed
in what he does.

What does it mean to be a hearer of the Word rather than a
"doer"? Give some practical examples.

When have you been "a forgetful hearer"? What caused you to
forget? How can you avoid forgetting God's Word in the future?

If we were to reduce what James says in this passage to a formula, it would be likely be:

Instruction + Involvement = Spiritual Growth

We are going to take a close look at what it means to be instructed in this lesson, and at what it means to be involved in the next lesson.

Instruction

Instruction is required at every stage of spiritual growth. You needed to be instructed about Jesus Christ—His life and His atoning, sacrificial death—when you were in a state of unbelief. You needed to be instructed about your need for forgiveness and about God's plan for salvation. At each stage of your spiritual growth, you needed God's information about what you were experiencing, why you were experiencing it, and what a godly response should be to your experience. Instruction is absolutely vital for moving from one stage of spiritual growth to the next.

Throughout the Gospels, we find Jesus instructing His disciples and others. Jesus instructed Nicodemus about his need to be born again and about what it means to believe in God's Son (see John 3:1–21). Jesus instructed a woman who came to the well at Sychar about what it means to drink of living water and about how to worship God (see John 4:5–26). Jesus taught in parables, which are instructional stories that have a lesson of faith imbedded in them. Jesus engaged in numerous instructional sessions with His disciples, explaining to them the meaning of His parables and answering their questions. Jesus' disciples called Him "Rabbi" or "Rabboni," which means "Teacher." One of the greatest and longest pieces of instruction in all the Bible is a passage of Scripture that we call the Sermon on the Mount (see Matt. 5–7).

The epistles of Paul, Peter, and John are words of instruction, both to individuals in ministry and to the church as a whole. In Ephesians 4:11, we read that one of the main offices in the church is to be that of pastor-teacher. God has given us His Word to instruct us. The questions that we must ask ourselves are these: Am I willing to learn? Am I eager to be taught?

> Therefore I speak to them in parables, because seeing they do not see, and hearing they do not hear, nor do they understand.

> —Matthew 13:13

When have you deliberately refused to see or hear the truth? Why did you choose to stop your ears and eyes? What resulted?

What is required of a person if he is to hear and see God's truth? How does James' mirror analogy (James 1:21–25) fit into this process?

Two Types of Hearers

Hearing is a significant part of instruction—not merely hearing with the ears, but hearing with "spiritual" ears, which means actively hearing the meaning and the truth of what is being said. Jesus said repeatedly, "He who has ears to hear, let him hear!" (Matt. 11:15; 13:9; 13:43; Mark 4:9; 4:23; 7:16; Luke 8:8; 14:35). James identified two distinct types of hearers: careless and careful.

The Careless Hearer

The careless hearer is:

deceived. Many people falsely believe that, if they hear, they understand. Hearing is not the same as knowing or understanding. It is not the same as growing, having, or experiencing. Hearing by itself is not an automatic reception of a message, neither is it automatically productive. We must pay close attention to what we hear and then do something with it to gain genuine understanding. In other words, true hearing requires obedience.

distracted. The distracted hearer hears, seems to comprehend, but then immediately forgets what he hears because he becomes distracted by other concerns or by new information. Many Christians are like that when it comes to last Sunday's sermon! They will tell you that it was a good sermon and they felt blessed by it, but they can't recall a thing that was actually said! Hearing requires that we focus our attention and engage our memory. We must choose to remember what we hear so that we can apply it.

idle. James also states that there are those who hear and comprehend, but they never apply what they hear. To be a genuine *hearer* of the Word, we must become *doers* of the Word. We must apply what we hear; we must obey what we are taught.

Jesus cited some of the things that cause a person to be a careless hearer. In explaining His parable of the sower to His disciples, Jesus said:

When anyone hears the word of the kingdom, and does not understand it, then the wicked one comes and snatches away what was sown in his heart. This is he who received seed by the wayside. But he who received the seed on stony places, this is he who hears the word and immediately receives it with joy; yet he has no root in himself, but endures only for a while. For when tribulation or persecution arises because of the word, immediately he stumbles. Now he who received seed among the thorns is he who hears the word, and the cares of this world and the deceitfulness of riches choke the word, and he becomes unfruitful. But he who received seed on the good ground is he who hears the word and understands it, who indeed bears fruit and produces: some a hundredfold, some sixty, some thirty."

—Matthew 13:19–23

Define below the four types of soils that Jesus described, and explain in your own words what type of hearer each represents.

Wayside:

Stony:

Thorns:

Good ground:

✎ What is required of a hearer if he is to understand what he hears?

The Careful Hearer

The careful hearer is one who:

✎ **is intentional.** The careful hearer, James says, concentrates or focuses on what he hears. He is intentional about hearing—he wants to hear and he wants to be able to act on what he hears. He actively engages his memory to remember what he hears.

✎ **abides by what is heard.** The careful hearer attaches importance to what he hears from God's Word and immediately applies it to his life. He knows that he has heard truth and he eagerly seeks ways in which to express truth. He not only wants to *know* what is right; he wants to *do* what is right in God's eyes.

Jesus answered and said to him, "If anyone loves Me, he will keep My word; and My Father will love him, and We will come to him and make Our home with him. He who does not love Me does not keep My words; and the word which you hear is not Mine but the Father's who sent Me."

—John 14:23, 24

❧ What does it mean to keep Jesus' Word? What parts of Jesus' Word are you not keeping at present? What will you do about it this coming week?

❧ Why does Jesus equate obedience with loving God? How is disobedience actually a symptom of *not* loving God?

Recalling the Truth to Your Mind

Another key aspect of instruction is memory. To be truly instructed, we must perceive, comprehend, understand, and apply what we hear, but we must also choose to remember what we have learned. We must actively choose to recall what we have been taught.

Time and again through the Scriptures, the Israelites needed to remind themselves of God's deeds and the truth of God's Word to them. Recalling the truth to their minds nearly always led to a renewed trust in the Lord or to more active repentance. The same is true for us: the more we recall God's work in our hearts, the stronger we grow in our faith and the more eager we are to respond to God's directions. We must never forget the goodness of God or His promises to us.

There are two things that we can do to keep what we have learned active and alive in our minds.

1. Memorize God's Word

Commit God's Word to memory. One of the easiest ways to memorize God's Word is to write a verse on a three-by-five card and carry it with you, reading the verse *aloud* several dozen times over the course of a few days. You will be reading the verse with your eyes, but you will also be hearing it with your ears, which creates a double impact on your memory. After reading the verse several times, try reciting it from memory. Check your accuracy. Read the verse again a couple of times. This is a great way to make use of time spent driving, or the time that you spend waiting in airports, for appointments, or for others.

The Lord has said that the Holy Spirit will recall to our minds the words of Jesus when we need them for guidance, courage, or witnessing (see John 15:26, 27; 16:1–3). In order for the Lord to recall something to our minds, we must first have planted it *in* our minds. Routinely reading and memorizing God's Word is of great benefit to every believer, no matter how mature he may be.

> And these words which I command you today shall be in your heart. You shall teach them diligently to your children, and shall talk of them when you sit in your house, when you walk by the way, when you lie down, and when you rise up. You shall bind them as a sign on your hand, and they shall be as frontlets between your eyes. You shall write them on the doorposts of your house and on your gates.
>
> —Deuteronomy 6:6–9

✎ Most of us do not wear "frontlets" (phylacteries) on our foreheads, so give some practical examples of ways that one might apply these steps of memorizing God's Word today.

❧ Why did God include teaching one's children in the list of ways to memorize His Word? How does this help you remember His Word? How does it help your children?

2. Include God's Word in Your Praise and Prayers

Praise and thank God daily for what He has done for you—and do so in the context of reciting Scripture back to the Lord. For example, you might say, "Thank you, Lord, for providing what I needed yesterday. Your Word that 'all things shall be added unto you' has been proved true once again!"

Pray the Scriptures. For example, you might pray, "Lord, I am so grateful for your Word that says, 'I am the vine and you are the branches . . . without Me you can do nothing.' I believe that with all my heart, Lord, and I am trusting You today to reveal to me what I should say and do. I praise You that, as I follow the leading of Your Spirit, I will do and say those things that are of eternal benefit."

The more you relate your life to the Scriptures and the Scriptures to your life, the more your mind will be filled with the truth of God's Word, and the more the Holy Spirit can use the Word to instruct you on a daily basis.

How can a young man cleanse his way? By taking heed according to Your word. With my whole heart I have sought You; Oh, let me not wander from Your commandments! Your word I have hidden in my heart, that I might not sin against You.

—Psalm 119:9–11

When has God's Word come into your mind, preventing you from sin or leading you to make a good decision? When have you remembered His Word *after* making a bad decision?

Spend time this week memorizing Psalm 119:9–11.

Psalm 119 has often been called the "teaching and learning" psalm. It gives very specific instructions about how to receive spiritual truth into your life. I encourage you to read it fully and carefully. Note especially:

&. The Lord gives His blessing to those who know and keep His commandments (v. 2).

&. We are called to meditate on the Lord's precepts and to contemplate the Lord's ways (v. 15).

&. As we "run the course" of God's commandments, the Lord enlarges our hearts (v. 32).

&. Instruction produces "good judgment" as well as knowledge (v. 66).

&. Meditating on God's Word makes a person wiser than his enemies (v. 98).

&. We are called to *know* God's Word and to speak it (v. 172).

&. List below other insights about Scripture memory which you find in Psalm 119. What are some of the benefits? What are some helpful tips?

✿ Today and Tomorrow ✿

TODAY: UNDERSTANDING GOD'S WORD REQUIRES FIRST THAT I OBEY IT.

TOMORROW: I WILL WORK THIS WEEK ON MEMORIZING PSALM 119:9–11.

✿ Notes and Prayer Requests: ✿

God's Formula for Spiritual Growth (Part 2)

◈ In This Lesson ◈

LEARNING: WHAT DOES THIS "OBEDIENCE FORMULA" MEAN IN PRACTICAL TERMS?

GROWING: HOW SHOULD I RESPOND TO PEOPLE WHO HATE ME?

We are called to be doers of what we learn from God's Word (see James 1:22). But how do we become doers? What is required for us to be adequate "doers"? James gives us God's formula for spiritual growth:

INSTRUCTION + INVOLVEMENT = SPIRITUAL GROWTH

Doers are those who become involved with other people in doing God's work. We are never called to do God's work in isolation. We are always called to do God's work in association with others who are of like mind and heart.

Throughout the New Testament, we have numerous references to Christians being the body of Christ. Our relationship with others is described as that of a family. The work of the Lord is done in a community context, each believer contributing his unique talents and spiritual gifts to the body as a whole. In this way, the gospel is spread, the needs of God's people are met, and we individually experience greater joy, love, and purpose. The process results in mutual edification. To be part of a body or a family requires one thing from us: involvement.

Involvement

Instruction, the first half of the formula for spiritual growth, may be highly personal and individualized. We learn at different rates, each of us finding unique and personal ways in which to apply what we learn. But involvement requires that we develop relationships with other people. It is in the context of relationships that we *do* what we learn from God's Word. Our doing may involve tasks, but far more important, our doing involves people.

Many Christians take the approach, "I'm an idea person," or "I'm task-oriented"—and they then conclude, "I'm just not a people person." The truth of God's Word is that we are all called to become "people persons." We are to be involved with other people.

Let me remind you of several familiar passages of Scripture. Note that each of these is stated in "we," "our," or other group terms. (Italics have been added for emphasis.)

> *Our* Father in heaven, hallowed be Your name. Your kingdom come. Your will be done on hearth as it is in heaven. Give *us* this day our daily bread. And forgive us *our* debts, as we forgive *our* debtors.

> —Matthew 6:9–12

The harvest truly is plentiful, but the *laborers* are few.

—Matthew 9:37

Assuredly, I say to you, unless you are converted and become as little *children*, you will by no means enter the kingdom of heaven.

—Matthew 18:3

When Jesus sent out His disciples to preach the good news, heal the sick, and deliver those who were possessed by demons, He sent them out two by two (see Mark 6:7).

Why did Jesus use plurals ("us," "our") in the Lord's Prayer? Why did He send out his disciples in pairs, rather than singly? What does this teach about being involved with others?

The hallmark challenge of Jesus about service was this: "Whoever desires to be first among you, let him be your slave—just as the Son of Man did not come to be served, but to serve, and to give His life a ransom for many" (Matt. 20:27, 28). Jesus served others and poured out His life for many, and so we are to serve and pour out our life, energy, resources, time, and talents to meet the needs of others.

A Threefold Involvement

The involvement that we are to have with others is threefold:

1. *The Great Commandment: Love others.* Our supreme involvement with others is rooted in love.

> Jesus said to him, *"You shall love the Lord your God with all your heart, with all your soul, and with all your mind."* This is the first and great commandment. And the second is like it: *"You shall love your neighbor as yourself."* On these two commandments hang all the Law and the Prophets.
>
> —Matthew 22:37–40

Love is expressed by giving. We give our time, resources, talents, encouraging words, comforting presence, listening ears, watchful eyes—we give our gifts and our prayers. And we give with the intent of blessing, of meeting needs, and of building up those to whom we give. We give as the Lord commands us to give: generously, freely, sacrificially, and with a cheerful heart. We are called to literally "spend ourselves" in service to others.

95

∾ In Matthew 22:37–40 above, how are the two commandments (love God, love others) related to one another? In what ways is one not possible without the other?

∾ What did Jesus mean by, "On these two commandments hang all the Law and the Prophets"? In what sense does our entire obedience depend upon our love for God and others?

∾ Why did Jesus say "love your neighbor as yourself," rather than "love yourself and then your neighbor"? What is the difference? What is implied by Jesus' words?

2. *The Great Commission: Witness to others.* Our involvement is not to be limited to those who are in the body of Christ; rather, it is to include involvement with those who do not know the Lord so that we might lead sinners to believe in Jesus as their Savior and receive God's forgiveness of sin. Jesus said to His disciples then and now, "Go therefore and make disciples of all the nations, baptizing them in the name of the Father and of the Son and of the Holy Spirit, teaching them to observe all things that I have commanded you; and lo, I am with you always, even to the end of the age" (Matt. 28:19, 20).

To be an effective witness for Christ, we must let people know that we care about them and that we want them to be with us in heaven one day. We must love them as Christ loved them. Jesus gave very clear instructions about how we are to love even those who persecute us: Give to them, pray for them, and speak well of them (see Matt. 5:43, 44). In this, we establish an untarnished reputation of love and kindness, and our words about Christ have a far greater appeal.

You have heard that it was said, "*You shall love your neighbor* and hate your enemy." But I say to you, love your enemies, bless those who curse you, do good to those who hate you, and pray for those who spitefully use you and persecute you, that you may be sons of your Father in heaven; for He makes His sun rise on the evil and on the good, and sends rain on the just and on the unjust.

—Matthew 5:43–45

❧ Why does God send blessings on the good and the evil, the just and the unjust? What does this teach about His commands to love our enemies?

❧ Without naming names, list some experiences you've had with the following types of people, including how you responded to them.

Enemies:

Cursers:

Haters:

Spiteful users:

Persecutors:

3. *The Great Commitment:* Serving others. Jesus is our role model for service. On the night that He was betrayed, Jesus washed the feet of His disciples—doing the job of the lowliest household servant—and he said this about what He had done:

> "Do you know what I have done to you? You call Me Teacher and Lord, and you say well, for so I am. If I then, your Lord and Teacher, have washed your feet, you also ought to wash one another's feet. For I have given you an example, that you should do as I have done to you. Most assuredly, I say to you, a servant is not greater than his master; nor is he who is sent greater than he who sent him."

> —John 13:12–16

We are never to think ourselves too great, too important, too clean, too righteous, too intelligent, too wealthy, or too spiritual to undertake a task that will be a blessing to a person the Lord puts in our path. We are to give to all who ask of us—and to do so generously.

What does it mean to wash someone's feet in our culture today? Give some practical examples of work done by lowly servants.

≈ If you are not greater than Jesus, what sorts of service should you be willing to provide to others? What sort of attitude should you exhibit while serving?

How the Formula Works

James' formula for spiritual growth (INSTRUCTION + INVOLVEMENT = SPIRITUAL GROWTH) works in this way. The more we hear God's Word as careful hearers, diligent in our search for God's meaning and truth, and eager to remember God's Word and to apply it to our daily lives, the more we will actually apply God's Word.

The more we apply God's Word to our lives, putting it to the test and "trying it out," the more we discover that God's Word *works*. Others around us are affected in two ways. They are the recipients of our godly behavior, including our godly speech. Those who are influenced for good by what we do and say are likely to ask us what motivates us to do good. This gives us an opportunity to witness about the love and forgiveness and personal presence of the Lord in our lives. We grow spiritually as we share our faith.

Or, those around us may be influenced by our behavior to engage in godly behavior themselves, adopting godly attitudes or displaying godly speech. As they put God's truth into practical effect in their lives, they will also discover that it works, and they will want to continue to do good.

The more that we see God's truth as practical and producing a blessing in our lives, the more eager we will be to learn even more about God's ways, plans, and purposes. And the more we learn, the more we will want to apply God's truth. The cycle continues and builds, and what we do and say influences others in an ever-widening circle of influence and witness. As part of this process, we *grow* spiritually, and we find ourselves drawing closer and closer to the heart of God.

> But when you do a charitable deed, do not let your left hand know what your right hand is doing, that your charitable deed may be in secret; and your Father who sees in secret will Himself reward you openly.
>
> —Matthew 6:3, 4

What does it mean, in practical terms, to not let your left hand know what your right hand is doing? How is this done? Why is it important?

～ When have you done something good, then told others about it? What was the result? When have you *not* told others? How did that result differ?

The Lord promises a great blessing to those who seek to grow spiritually. Not only does He promise us His infinite and awesome presence, but He promises to meet our deepest needs. The more our needs are met, the greater our appreciation and love for God will grow. And the greater our love for God grows, the more we delight in spending time with Him. God is no longer a far-off stranger to us; rather, He becomes our nearest and dearest Friend and the One on whom we rely for unconditional love, acceptance, and fellowship.

> No longer do I call you servants, for a servant does not know what his master is doing; but I have called you friends, for all things that I heard from My Father I have made known to you.
>
> —John 15:15

❧ What is the difference between a servant and a friend? How do you tend to treat friends differently from those who serve you, such as a waitress or a cab driver?

❧ Why did Jesus equate friendship with telling others what His Father had told Him? What sort of intimacy does this suggest? How does it apply to the ways that you treat others?

Today and Tomorrow

TODAY: JAMES' "OBEDIENCE FORMULA" MEANS LOVING OTHERS, SERVING OTHERS, AND WITNESSING TO OTHERS.

TOMORROW: I WILL PRAYERFULLY LOOK FOR WAYS TO LOVE AND SERVE OTHERS THIS WEEK, SHARING THE GOSPEL WHENEVER GOD GIVES ME AN OPPORTUNITY.

Notes and Prayer Requests:

Time Apart with the Lord

There is one final key to spiritual growth that is perhaps the greatest secret of all. It certainly is a factor in every stage of spiritual growth. It is perhaps the foremost factor that gives rise to all requirements for spiritual growth. The key is this: spending time alone with the Lord.

King David has been called a "man after God's own heart." To be a man *after* God's own heart means that David needed first to know the mind and heart of God so that he might be and do what the Lord desired of him. David sought to know God. He frequently "inquired" of the Lord. He spent time in the Lord's presence singing to Him from the depths of his heart. In 2 Samuel 7:18 we read:

> Then King David went in and sat before the LORD; and he said: "Who am I, O Lord GOD? And what is my house, that You have brought me this far?"

What does it mean for David to "sit" before the Lord? It means that he spent time alone in the presence of the Lord, communicating with Him from the depths of his heart, asking questions of God, and listening quietly before the Lord for His answers.

What is the essence of David's question in this prayer, in your own words?

Spend time right now in praise and thanksgiving to the Lord for the blessings which He has bestowed in your life.

Jesus frequently sought time apart with His heavenly Father. Time with the Father was a source of comfort and strength to Him. Jesus also sought time alone with His disciples so that He might teach them and they might be refreshed spiritually (see Luke 9:10). When we spend time with the Lord, we are wise to spend this time alone with Him, in a place where we will not be distracted or interrupted, for a period of time sufficient for us to relax completely and focus our attention fully upon the Lord and His Word. We must be willing to wait in the Lord's presence until we receive God's directions or His words of comfort and edification.

✎ When is the best time for you to spend alone with God? Where do you find it most effective to do so?

✎ What sorts of things tend to interrupt or hinder your times with God? What techniques have you found effective in combating those distractions?

Why People Don't Spend Time with God

There are a number of reasons that people don't desire to spend time alone with God. The foremost reason is that they aren't sure of their relationship with God and, therefore, they are afraid of God. Those who are born again have a Father-child relationship with the Lord. Our heavenly Father loves us unconditionally and is tender and patient in His dealings with us. If we do not perceive God in this manner, however, we tend to avoid Him and are fearful of spending time alone in His presence. If you are reluctant to spend time apart with the Lord, consider these questions. Do you perceive God as:

- loving or demanding?
- near or distant?
- patient or intolerant?
- gentle or angry?
- understanding or insensitive?
- generous or stingy?
- faithful or inconsistent?

What you believe about God will determine the amount of time that you spend with Him, and the attitude that you have toward God when you are in His presence.

Come to Me, all you who labor and are heavy laden, and I will give you rest. Take My yoke upon you and learn from Me, for I am gentle and lowly in heart, and you will find rest for your souls.

—Matthew 11:28, 29

What does it mean, in practical terms, to be "lowly of heart"? How is this quality surprising to find in the Creator of the Universe? What are the implications of this in your life?

What does it mean to take Christ's yoke upon yourself? How is this done? How can wearing a yoke (used on oxen when plowing) actually provide a person with rest?

The Blessings of Time Alone with God

The Bible speaks of many great blessings that come from spending time alone with the Lord. Those who spend time alone with the Lord find comfort, hope, and joy in His presence. They find themselves being built up, from the inside out, and they generally emerge from a time with the Lord feeling refreshed and more courageous as they face their needs or tackle their problems. As you read the passage below from Psalms, note the very specific rewards of meditation—which for the Christian may be defined as quiet contemplation about God's Word in God's presence:

Oh, how I love Your law! It is my meditation all the day. You, through Your commandments, make me wiser than my enemies; for they are ever with me. I have more understanding than all my teachers, for Your testimonies are my meditation. I understand more than the ancients, because I keep Your precepts. I have restrained my feet from every evil way, that I may keep Your word. I have not departed from Your judgments, for You Yourself have taught me. How sweet are Your words to my taste, sweeter than honey to my mouth! Through Your precepts I get understanding; therefore I hate every false way.

—Psalm 119:97–104

᠅ List below the rewards of meditating on God's Word listed in these verses.

꙾ When has God's Word tasted sweet to you? How can a person keep that sweetness fresh, rather than becoming dull and uninterested toward God's Word?

What Do We Do?

There are four helpful things that you can do as you spend time apart with the Lord. These are things that can lead to your hearing the voice of God in fresh, invigorating ways.

1. Review the Past

As David sat in the presence of the Lord, he no doubt remembered his fight with Goliath, his years of successfully avoiding Saul's murderous intent, and the battles that he had won. In the passage that we noted above, David had just heard from the prophet Nathan that the Lord was going to establish his house, his kingdom, and his throne forever (see 2 Sam. 7:16, 17). David no doubt reviewed God's many blessings to him in the past as he weighed these wonderful words from God.

As you sit in the Lord's presence, reflect on all that the Lord has done for you, in you, and through you. David wrote:

> Enter into His gates with thanksgiving, and into His courts with praise. Be thankful to Him, and bless His name. For the LORD is good; His mercy is everlasting, and His truth endures to all generations.

> —Psalm 100:4, 5

What does it mean to enter the gates and courts of God? How is this done in your life?

Make a list below of blessings that God has bestowed in your life, then spend time each day for the next week giving Him thanks.

2. Reflect upon God

Spend time reflecting upon the awesome nature of God. Especially focus on His greatness, His grace to you, and His goodness. Spend time contemplating the many names of God and Jesus in the Scriptures; each name reflects a facet of the Lord's nature. Consider these attributes of God:

Eternal	Loving
Faithful	Merciful
Good	All-Powerful (Omnipotent)
Gracious	All-Wise (Omniscient)
Holy	Ever-Present (Omnipresent)
Immutable	Righteous
Jealous	Sovereign
Just	Long-suffering

Our problems will seem smaller and smaller the more we put our attention on our great, awesome, and loving God—who sent His only begotten Son to die for our sins so that we might be reconciled to Him and live with Him forever in heaven.

Through the LORD's mercies we are not consumed, because His compassions fail not. They are new every morning; great is Your faithfulness. "The LORD is my portion," says my soul, "Therefore I hope in Him!" The LORD is good to those who wait for Him, to the soul who seeks Him. It is good that one should hope and wait quietly for the salvation of the LORD.

—Lamentations 3:22–26

❧ When have you felt as though life's problems were going to consume you? How did you respond in those situations?

❧ What does it mean to "wait quietly for the salvation of the Lord"? How is this done? Why is it vitally important?

3. Remember God's Promises

God has made numerous promises throughout His Word regarding your provision, protection, and potential to receive His blessings. As you spend time with the Lord, thank Him for His promises even as you recount them and reread them aloud. Allow God's promises to kindle your faith—for surely what God has said, God will do. He is faithful at all times to His own Word!

> His divine power has given to us all things that pertain to life and godliness, through the knowledge of Him who called us by glory and virtue, by which have been given to us exceedingly great and precious promises, that through these you may be partakers of the divine nature, having escaped the corruption that is in the world through lust.
>
> —2 Peter 1:3, 4

List below some things that you feel "pertain to life and godliness." Be realistic and practical.

List below some of the "great and precious promises" from Scripture which pertain to the list above.

4. Make Requests of the Lord Regarding Your Spiritual Growth

Spend time alone with the Lord, thanking Him for His many acts of mercy and kindness in the past, reflecting upon His goodness and love, and remembering His promises. Then, ask the Lord for those things that you desire the most. The Lord delights in answering petitions such as these. Ask Him to:

- give you His perspective on your problems, relationships, and opportunities.
- give you His peace.
- give you a positive attitude and to help you forgive those who may have hurt you, rejected you, or disappointed you.
- purify your thoughts.
- give you a passion to obey Him.
- direct all of your steps.

And Then, Listen

Most important as you spend time alone with the Lord: listen. Simply sit quietly in the Lord's presence and allow Him to speak to you. So often we come into the Lord's presence and we do nothing but talk. Our praises, thanksgiving, and reading of Scripture are right things to speak to the Lord, but it is also right that we wait quietly in His presence. Psalm 46:10 wisely admonishes us, "Be still, and know that I am God."

The Lord delights in speaking to the willing heart. He delights in "growing us up" into the likeness of His Son. He delights in revealing to us His plan and purpose for our lives. He delights in encouraging us with

His presence, empowering us to do His will, and embracing us tenderly when we need His comfort. Choose to spend time alone with the Lord. Truly there is no more important way to spend your time!

> I am God, and there is no other; I am God, and there is none like Me, declaring the end from the beginning, and from ancient times things that are not yet done, saying, "My counsel shall stand, and I will do all My pleasure," calling a bird of prey from the east, the man who executes My counsel, from a far country. Indeed I have spoken it; I will also bring it to pass. I have purposed it; I will also do it.
>
> —Isaiah 46:9–11

☙ Spend some time now in prayer. Ask the Lord to speak to you—then sit quietly and listen, keeping your mind free from clutter and worldly pressures.

The Lord Desires Your Presence

We said at the outset of this book that the Lord has issued a wonderful invitation to each of us to come into His presence and to grow into His likeness. The Lord's desire is that you might know Him, love Him, serve Him, and live with Him forever. The Lord's desire is to have an intimate, personal relationship with you.

As is appropriate with many invitations, a response is requested from you. What will your response be today? Will you accept God's invitation? Will you choose to grow in your relationship with Him until you experience genuine intimacy with Christ, your Creator and Savior and Lord?

❧ Today and Tomorrow ❧

TODAY: GOD HAS SENT ME AN INVITATION TO MEET WITH HIM EACH DAY, AND I WILL ACCEPT HIS INVITATION.

TOMORROW: I WILL SET ASIDE A REGULAR TIME EACH DAY THIS WEEK TO MEET ALONE WITH GOD.

⤫ Notes and Prayer Requests: ⤫

Notes and Prayer Requests:

❦ Notes and Prayer Requests: ❦

⤬ **Notes and Prayer Requests:** ⤬

The Life Principles Series

STUDY GUIDES

Other Books by Charles Stanley